Foods of Peru

Barbara Sheen

KIDHAVEN PRESS
A part of Gale, Cengage Learning

GALE
CENGAGE Learning™

Detroit • New York • San Francisco • New Haven, Conn • Waterville, Maine • London

LIBRARY OF CONGRESS CATALOGING-IN-PUBLICATION DATA

Sheen, Barbara.
  Foods of Peru / by Barbara Sheen.
    p. cm. -- (A taste of culture)
  Includes bibliographical references and index.
  ISBN 978-0-7377-5346-2 (hardcover)
  1. Food habits--Peru--Juvenile literature. 2. Food--Peru--Juvenile literature. 3. Peru--Social life and customs--Juvenile literature. I. Title.
  GT2853.P4S54 2011
  394.1'20985--dc22

                                                                    2010032959

Kidhaven Press
27500 Drake Rd.
Farmington Hills MI 48331

ISBN-13: 978-0-7377-5346-2
ISBN-10: 0-7377-5346-3

Printed in the United States of America
1 2 3 4 5 6 7 14 13 12 11 10

Printed by Bang Printing, Brainerd, MN, 1st Ptg., 10/2010

Contents

A Diverse Land

Peru is a land of contrasts. Within its borders are snowcapped mountains, great rivers, huge lakes, vast deserts, high-altitude cloud forests, tropical rainforests, windswept plains, fertile valleys, and sandy beaches that meet the Pacific Ocean. In fact, 89 of the world's 104 ecosystems, places where living and nonliving things interact, are found in Peru.

Peru's diverse landscape provides its people with an abundant supply of food. Its markets overflow with fruits, vegetables, seafood, and meats. Peruvian cooks take advantage of this bounty. Yet, there are four staples—potatoes, corn, chili peppers, and seafood—that Peruvian cooks cannot do without. These ingredients

Ancient Civilizations

Peru was the home of many advanced ancient civilizations. One of the first was the Chinchero culture (6000 BC). This group mummified its dead long before the ancient Egyptians did.

The Chavin culture (1200–400 BC) was another advanced group. These people built the Chavin de Huantar temple in the Peruvian Andes, which is known for its sophisticated engineering.

The Moche (200–700 AD) and Nasca (300–800 AD) cultures arose next. The Moche built great temples. The Nasca etched huge permanent geometric and animal symbols into the desert, known as the Nasca Lines.

Next, came the Inca Empire (1200–1532 AD). The Peruvian city of Cusco was the Incan capital. The Inca also built Machu Pichu (MAH-chu PEE-chu), a magnificent city in the Andes Mountains, which is a tourist site today. The Inca were highly organized and had a sophisticated farming and economic system. They also had a strong army. Their empire extended from Colombia to Chile, an area larger than that of the Roman Empire.

have played a major role in the Peruvian people's diet for thousands of years.

Thousands of Varieties

Peru has a long history. It is one of the world's great centers of ancient civilizations. The ruins of ancient **pre-Columbian** cities dot the landscape. Potatoes, which originated in Peru, have nourished civilizations here for 8,000 years.

Nearly 4,000 varieties of potatoes grow in Peru, each with its own taste, shape, and color.

Worldwide, there are about 5,000 varieties of potatoes. Almost 4,000 of these, in every size and color imaginable, grow in Peru. Most Peruvian supermarkets have two entire aisles just of potatoes.

"Here," explains Peruvian Guillermo Payet, "are countless baskets of potatoes—red, fat, black and bright orange with pink spots."[1] Each type tastes different. They can be sweet, tart, bitter, creamy, sticky, starchy, waxy, hearty, or delicate.

Peruvians eat potatoes at almost every meal, in much the same way as other cultures eat bread. They fry potatoes, turn them into pies and brightly colored potato chips, roast them, bake them, boil them, put them in salads, and top them with cheese and spicy sauces.

They layer cold yellow or blue mashed potatoes with chicken, tuna, or shrimp salad to make causa Limeña (CAH-ooh-sah lee-MAY-nyah), a popular lunch dish. And, they freeze-dry potatoes to make **chuño** (CHOON-yo), a traditional Peruvian specialty.

Chuño may be the earliest form of freeze-dried food. The **Inca**, Peruvian Indians who ruled over a vast South American empire from the 13th to 16th centuries, began making it as a way to preserve potatoes. The process required leaving the potatoes outside where they were exposed to freezing nighttime temperatures and intense sunlight during the day. This cycle, which lasted about five days, caused the potatoes to dry out, harden, and shrink until they looked like small white stones.

The dried potatoes could be kept for months without spoiling. When they were soaked in water, they

In its preserved state chuño resembles small white stones. Once it is rehydrated, however, chuño cooks and tastes much like any other potato.

Peruvian Potato Salad

This is a simple Peruvian-style potato salad. It can be served hot or cold. In Peru, the chili in the recipe would be ají amarillo. It is hard to find in North America. This recipe uses a serrano pepper instead. Any medium-hot red, yellow, or green chili pepper such as jalapeño or Big Jim chili would work.

Ingredients
2 medium potatoes, peeled and cut into chunks
1 large tomato, diced
1 serrano chili pepper, seeded and diced
1 tablespoon olive oil
1 tablespoon red wine vinegar
1 teaspoon cilantro, chopped
salt and pepper to taste.

Directions
1. Put the potatoes in a pot. Cover them with cold water. Cook over medium heat, bringing the water to a boil. Cook until the potatoes are soft. Drain the potatoes well.
2. Put all the ingredients in a bowl and mix well.
Serves 2.

softened and rehydrated. Then, they were cooked much like any potato, or they were ground into flour. Chuño was so valuable to the Inca that they used the dried potatoes as a form of payment for their taxes.

Today chuño is available in cans. It is a key ingredient in carapulcra (cah-rah-POOL-crah), a tasty stew that Peruvians have been eating for centuries.

Choclo

Corn, or **choclo** (CHOH-cloh), as it is known in Peru, was also an important part of the Incan diet. More than that, the Inca revered corn. One of their most important gods was the Corn God. Corn was so vital to Incan lives that their chief, who was believed to be descended from the gods, planted the first corn seeds himself every year.

Corn is still important to Peruvians. One hundred fifty varieties of corn, in every color of the rainbow, grow here. That is more than anywhere else on Earth. Peruvians boil, steam, roast, bake, grind, dry, and pop corn. In fact, popcorn originated in Peru.

Fried kernels of corn and ears of whole steamed corn are favorite snacks all over Peru.

According to

Street vendors across Peru can be found selling steamed ears of corn.

Peruvian writer Alvaro Ruiz de Somocurcio, "There is nothing more exquisite to eat than steamed corn, soft, toasted and sweet, accompanied with a slice of fresh cheese."[2]

Corn is also the chief ingredient in casseroles, stews, soups, savory pies, jellies, desserts, and beverages. Inchi cache (EEN-chee CAH-chay), a stew made with chicken, roasted bright-yellow corn, and peanuts, is a popular dish. Chicha morada (CHEE-chah mor-AH-dah), a refreshing drink made with purple corn is another colorful favorite. And, chicha, beer made from fermented corn, has been a popular Peruvian alcoholic drink for centuries.

Measuring a Pepper's Heat

Chili peppers contain a chemical called capsaicin that makes them hot. The more capsaicin in a chili pepper, the hotter it is. To determine a pepper's heat, food scientists use units called Scoville units. These units represent the amount of capsaicin a particular type of chili contains.

Units range from zero to over 1 million. The hottest pepper in the world, the bhut jolokia, also known as a ghost chili, comes from India and contains over 1 million Scoville units. The Mexican red habanero chili is the second hottest. It contains about 500,000 Scoville units. By comparison, ají amarillo contains about 30,000 units, while bell peppers contain zero.

The Color of the Sun

Ají (ah-HEE), or chili peppers, are another ancient and indispensable part of Peruvian cooking. They brighten already-colorful Peruvian dishes, and give everything a fresh, zesty flavor. The hot peppers have been part of the Peruvian diet since 8000 BC. Archaeologists have found their remains in caves, and drawings of them on ancient pottery.

Three hundred different varieties of chili peppers grow here, each with its own unique size, shape, color, and heat intensity. The most popular is ají amarillo (ah-HEE ah-mah-REE-yo), or yellow chili. These long, slender peppers have a delicate, spicy flavor. Their brilliant-yellow color, which turns deep orange as

The majority of Peruvian dishes contain some variety of chili peppers.

it matures, gives many Peruvian dishes a distinctive sunny hue. Ají amarillo is so popular that bowls of **salsa** (SAHL-sah), or sauce made with the peppers combined with onions, lime juice, and spices, are served with almost every meal. Diners add the sauce to anything and everything.

"Just add a little ají to soups, stews, meats, or cebiches [a raw seafood dish] to give a wonderful kick to the food,"[3] says author Maria Baez Kijac.

Peruvian cooks not only use the peppers in salsa, they add sliced fresh peppers to salads, stews, and fish dishes. They bake them stuffed with shrimp and cheese. And, they grind them into a paste or powder, which they use as seasoning. There are few Peruvian dishes

Salsa Criolla

Salsa criolla is a popular Peruvian sauce. It can be used as a dip or added to food as a spice. Peruvians usually use ají amarillo in this salsa. The following recipe contains jalapeño peppers, which are easier to find in North America.

Ingredients
2 jalapeño peppers, seeded and minced
1 small red onion, diced
juice of 1 large lime
1 teaspoon red wine vinegar
½ teaspoon garlic powder
2 tablespoons cilantro, chopped
salt and pepper to taste

Directions
1. Soak the onion in cold water for 20 minutes and drain.
2. Combine all the ingredients in a bowl and mix well.
3. Cover the bowl and refrigerate for about one hour.
Makes 1 cup.

Ají amarillo is traditionally used in this salsa recipe.

that do not contain chili peppers. Yet, Peruvian food is not overly spicy. Peruvians value chili peppers more for their delicate flavor than for their heat. In fact, most Peruvian cooks remove the peppers' veins and seeds and simmer them in water before adding them to recipes. This lessens their heat.

Seafood

Seafood, too, gives Peruvian foods delicate flavor. It has always played a key role in Peruvian life. The Humboldt Current, a cold, nutrient-rich ocean current that supports all sorts of marine life, flows off the coast of Peru. Peruvian coastal waters brim over with edible water creatures, as does the Amazon River, the second longest river in the world, which flows through Peru and Lake Titicaca (Tee-tee-CAH-cah), the world's highest lake, which is located on the border of Peru and Bolivia. Eels, scallops, shrimps, squid, mussels, octopuses, lobsters, piranhas, cod, sea bass, and red snapper are just a few of the hundreds of water creatures that inhabit Peruvian waters. More species of fish and shellfish are found in Peruvian waters than anywhere else on Earth.

With so much seafood readily available, it is not surprising that archaeologists, people who study ancient

With the close proximity of the Pacific Ocean and the Amazon River, fresh seafood is abundant in Peru.

cultures, have found piles of fish bones in the ruins of ancient villages and tombs. Ancient coastal people such as the Moche (MOH-chay) built little reed canoes for fishing, which in modern form are still used today. They ate fresh seafood morning, noon, and night. And, they preserved fish by smoking or sun-drying it. They took the preserved fish inland where they traded it with other tribes for **llama** wool.

For modern Peruvians, only the freshest seafood will do.

"The fish go from the sea to the kitchen to the table in rapid order,"[4] explains author Copeland Marks. The idea of eating day-old or frozen fish is unthinkable to Peruvians.

Fresh seafood is grilled, broiled, boiled, baked, fried, steamed, and eaten raw. It is turned into thick chowders and stews, thrown into omelets, steamed in banana leaves, featured in salads, and topped with spicy or creamy sauces. In Peru, according to Marks, "seafood is king, and so are the myriad [many] numbers of recipes. ... Peruvians can be thankful for the quantity, quality, and variety of their natural bounty from the sea."[5]

Peruvians can also be thankful for the many other fresh foods that abound here. Flavorful chili peppers, brightly colored corn and potatoes, and fresh seafood are among everyone's favorites. These ingredients have played an essential part in Peruvian life for thousands of years.

A Cultural Blend

Many different cultural groups have played a role in shaping Peru. Migrating tribal people first arrived in Peru more than 8,000 years ago. Historians say these people came from Asia or Polynesia, a group of islands in the South Pacific. They built great cities, pyramids, and irrigation canals, created beautiful works of art, and developed far-reaching trade networks and complex forms of government.

In 1532 Spanish **conquistador** Francisco Pizarro arrived, seeking gold and riches. He claimed Peru for Spain. Spanish settlers soon followed. They introduced many new foods to Peru. Many of the settlers intermarried with native Peruvians, creating a cultural group known as Cri-

The Columbian Exchange

The Columbian exchange is the name given to the interchange of animals, plants, culture, and diseases between Europe and the Americas, following Christopher Columbus's voyage in 1492.

The Europeans introduced to the Americas cattle, sheep, pigs, chickens, wheat, rice, onions, citrus fruit, sugarcane, coffee, olives, and grapes, among other food stuffs. They also brought horses, which became an important means of transportation for Native Americans, and a new religion, Christianity. Unfortunately, they also introduced diseases that were unknown to Native Americans, too. One such disease, smallpox, killed 200,000 Inca.

In exchange, the Europeans brought home such items as corn, potatoes, yams, tomatoes, chili peppers, strawberries, pumpkins, squash, various nuts, cocoa (a bean used to make chocolate), pineapple, and tobacco.

ollos (Cree-OH-yos), or Creoles. The Spanish and wealthy Creoles brought African slaves to Peru to work on vast plantations. When slavery ended, Chinese laborers were brought to Peru. Immigrants from other countries, such as Italy, France, and Japan, also made Peru their home.

Peruvian cooking is a mixture of the foods and cooking styles of these different groups. Favorite dishes such as **ceviche** (say-VEE-chay), lomo saltado (LOH-moh sahl-TAH-doh), ají de gallina (ah-HEE day gah-YEE-nah), and **cuy** (COO-ee) are delicious examples of this cultural blend.

Ceviche is one of Peru's most well known dishes.

Ceviche

Ceviche is Peru's national dish. It is made of cubes of raw fish or shellfish that are spiced with chili peppers, red onion, and salt, and marinated in lime juice for about a half hour. Acids in the lime juice change the look and texture of the fish turning it from pink to white, much like heat does, but the fish is not actually "cooked" in the same way as it is with heat.

Peruvians use only the freshest fish to make ceviche. Less-than-fresh fish and seafood tastes mushy and can cause food poisoning. But this is not a problem in Peru where, according to Claudia Reano, who grew up in Peru, "a fish will be cubed, marinated, and put in a bowl sometimes less than an hour after being caught."[6]

Peruvians have been making ceviche in some form

Ceviche

Ceviche can be made with any type of fresh fish or sea-food. Since eating raw fish presents a danger of food poisoning, the fish must be very fresh and not frozen. This minimizes but does not entirely eliminate the threat of food poisoning. Peruvians also make ceviche with mushrooms. One pound of sliced white mush-rooms can be substituted for fish. Lemon juice can be substituted for lime juice, or for a sweeter taste, use three-quarters of a cup of lime or lemon juice and a quarter cup orange juice.

Ingredients
1 pound white fish of choice (tilapia, sole, bass), rinsed and cut into
   1-inch chunks
1 small red onion, thinly sliced
1 tablespoon cilantro, chopped
1 jalapeño pepper, seeded and chopped
1 cup lime juice
1 tablespoon minced garlic
salt and pepper to taste

for thousands of years. Peru's earliest native people made ceviche by marinating fish and chilis in an acidic native fruit known as tumbo (TOOM-boh). The Spanish brought limes and onions to Peru, which were soon added to the recipe.

Ceviche tastes tart and spicy, and smells faintly of the sea. It is traditionally served on a bed of lettuce accompanied by a small piece of corn on the cob, a chunk of sweet potato, and boiled yuca, a starchy na-

Directions

1. Soak the onion in cold water for 20 minutes, then drain.
2. Mix the lime juice, garlic, chili pepper, onions, cilantro, and salt and pepper.
3. Put the fish in a bowl. Pour the juice mix over the fish. Make sure all the fish is covered. Cover the bowl and refrigerate for at least 2–3 hours. The fish is ready to eat when it has turned firm and opaque.
4. Serve ceviche on a lettuce leaf accompanied by corn, sweet potatoes, or avocado slices and crackers.

Serves 4.

Ceviche is shown here with a side of cancha.

tive vegetable. A bowl of cancha (CAHN-cha), a type of popcorn made from giant white corn kernels toasted in oil and salt, is served on the side. Peruvians often end the meal with tiger's milk, the juice that remains after the ceviche is eaten.

Cevicherias (say-vee-chay-REE-ahs), restaurants that specialize in ceviche, can be found all over Peru. They are a popular meeting place for hungry Peruvians who cannot get enough of their national dish.

A Touch of China

Lomo saltado is another national favorite. This color-ful dish consists of juicy slices of steak cooked with ají amarillo, tomatoes, and purple onions, seasoned with ginger and soy sauce, then topped with fried potatoes. It combines native Peruvian ingredients with beef, which was introduced to Peru by the Spanish, along with ginger and soy sauce, popular Chinese seasonings,

and the Chinese method of cooking food rapidly over high heat known as stir-frying.

Chinese immigrants began arriving in Peru in 1850. They came to work on railroads and plantations. By 1880, about 300,000 Chinese people were living in Peru. Eventually, many opened restaurants in which they combined fresh local foods with Chinese ingredients and cooking methods.

The results were wildly popular. Today, there are about 5,000 Chinese-Peruvian, or **chifa** (CHEE-fah), restaurants in Lima, Peru's capital. The food they serve is different from any other food in the world.

According to Peruvian writer Mariella Mazzei, "It is unique not only because of its authentic origin, but also due to its wonderful fusion of flavors, colors, exquisite aromas, textures and Chinese and Peruvian ingredients. ... Chinese cooks understood the richness of our popular kitchen and learned to prepare Peruvian dishes flavored with slight Asian touches."[7]

Chinese-Peruvian restaurants, or chifa, are very popular in Peru.

Lomo Saltado

Lomo saltado is not difficult to make. The french fries can be made by frying sliced potatoes in oil or using frozen french fries. Chicken can be substituted for beef. Peruvians use ají amarillo in lomo saltado. This recipe uses jalapeño pepper because it can be hard to find ají amarillo in North America.

Ingredients
1 pound beef tenderloin cut into thin slices
1 pound package frozen french fries
1 jalapeño pepper, seeded and chopped
1 red onion, sliced thin
3 salad tomatoes, sliced
1 tablespoon cilantro
1 tablespoon minced garlic
2 tablespoons soy sauce
1 tablespoon white vinegar
1 teaspoon ginger
2 tablespoons olive oil

European Influences

Ají de gallina, tender bits of shredded chicken cooked in creamy hot-pepper sauce, is another popular dish that reflects the different cultures that are part of Peru. It combines typical native ingredients such as chili peppers, nuts, and potatoes with chicken, which was brought to Peru by the Spanish, French cream sauce, and parmesan cheese, a contribution of the second

Directions

1. Put the meat in a bowl and cover with the vinegar, soy sauce, ginger, garlic, and cilantro.
2. Make the french fries according to the directions on the package.
3. Heat some oil in a pan or wok over high heat. Take the meat out of the marinade. Save the marinade. Put the meat in the pan and cook for about 2 minutes.
4. Add the other ingredients, including the marinade and cook until the onions and tomatoes are tender and the meat is cooked through.
5. Serve lomo saltado on top of rice and the french fries on top of the meat.

Serves 4.

Lomo saltado is a delicious combination of Peruvian and Chinese ingredients.

largest group after the Spanish to settle in Peru—Italian immigrants.

The French Revolution caused many French chefs who worked for French noblemen to lose their jobs after their employers were killed or jailed. Many of these chefs came to Peru in the early 19th century to cook for wealthy Creole families. They blended French-style cooking with local ingredients and recipes, creating new dishes like ají de gallina.

Ají de gallina is a Peruvian dish that incorporates French and Italian influences into its rich and creamy taste.

To make ají de gallina, chefs boil a chicken. When the chicken is cooked, they let it cool; then they shred it. Next, they make the sauce. To do so, they put white bread, milk or cream, walnuts, parmesan cheese, ají amarillo powder, fried onions, and garlic in a food processor and **puree** (pure-AY) the mixture until it turns to a thick, velvety sauce. The sauce is poured over the chicken and the whole thing is heated until it is piping hot.

Ají de gallina is usually served on a bed of rice, topped with slices of yellow potato, hard-boiled egg, and black olives. This bright-yellow dish tastes creamy, rich, spicy, and distinctively Peruvian.

Quinoa

Quinoa (KEEN-wah) is an ancient grain rich in protein, calcium, iron, and vitamin B. It has been cultivated in Peru for about 5,000 years. The Inca called quinoa "the mother grain." Balls of quinoa mixed with fat, called war balls, were a staple of Incan soldiers' diet. This food nourished the men on long marches.

When the Spanish arrived in Peru, they brought with them rice and wheat. These new grains caused quinoa's popularity to decrease in Peru. However, because of its high nutritional value, quinoa's popularity has again grown in recent years.

Depending on the variety, quinoa can be white, pink, red, brown, or black. It is usually cooked like rice, and has a mild nutty taste and texture. It can be substituted for rice in most dishes, and it is tasty in soups, stews, and casseroles. It is eaten cold in salads, used in cereals, and turned into flour.

Cuy

Guinea pig, or cuy, as it is called in Peru because of the sound the animal makes, is another Peruvian favorite. It has its roots in Peru's Andean communities, where the native people have raised guinea pigs for food for about 5,000 years. In fact, before the Spanish brought other forms of meat such as cattle, sheep, and pork to Peru, cuy was an important source of protein for Peru's native people. Many raised the little animals in their kitchens. The animals required little space, ate food

Historically cuy, or guinea pig, was an important source of protein for Peruvians because other forms of meat such as cattle, sheep, and pork were not native to the coastal nation.

scraps, and reproduced rapidly, ensuring a constant supply of meat. Cuy was so important to the Inca that the remains of the animals have been found entombed with Incan mummies. The Inca not only ate cuy, they used the animal's intestines for fortune-telling and the bones to diagnose disease.

Cuy is still very popular. Peruvians eat about 65 million guinea pigs per year. The animals are raised commercially in Peru, and many native families still raise them in their kitchens. Cuy are also raised in the kitchens of restaurants known as cuyerias (coo-ee-ay-REE-ahs) that specialize in making cuy.

North Americans who keep guinea pigs as pets may find the idea of eating the animals distasteful. Peruvians, however, look at it differently. They consider cuy a delicacy. Eating it is a part of their history and culture. The dish is so much a part of Peruvian culture that a painting in the cathedral in Cusco, Peru, depicts Jesus Christ and his disciples eating cuy.

The meat is prepared in a number of ways. Frying, a cooking method introduced by the Spanish, is among the most popular. Cuy chactado (chahk-TAH-doh) is a traditional favorite. To make it, a whole cuy is spread out like a butterfly, seasoned with salt, pepper, and garlic, then flattened under a stone and deep-fried until it is crisp and brown. Each diner gets one whole cuy, head and all, accompanied by fresh ají amarillo and potatoes. Cuy tastes similar to rabbit. By eating it, writer Matt Villano says he "had partaken in one of the most long-lasting culinary [food] traditions in Peruvian history."[8]

Popular dishes like cuy, ají de gallina, lomo saltado, and ceviche all reflect Peru's rich history and the many groups that have shaped the nation. These foods are a delicious blend of Peru's culture.

A Sweet Tooth

Most Peruvians love sweets. Peruvian street vendors offer delicious sweet treats that tempt passers-by. Little cafés and restaurants, too, serve up a wide range of sweet snacks and desserts. Among the most popular are fresh-fruit drinks, fruit-flavored ice cream, caramel-filled sandwich cookies named alfajores (al-fa-HO-rays), and picarónes (pee-cah-ROH-nays), hot fried pastries.

Fruit Treats

More than 600 different types of fruits grow wild in Peru's mountains and rainforest. Some, like pineapples, berries, and mangoes, are familiar to North Americans, while others like **lúcumas** (LOO-coo-mahs) are less

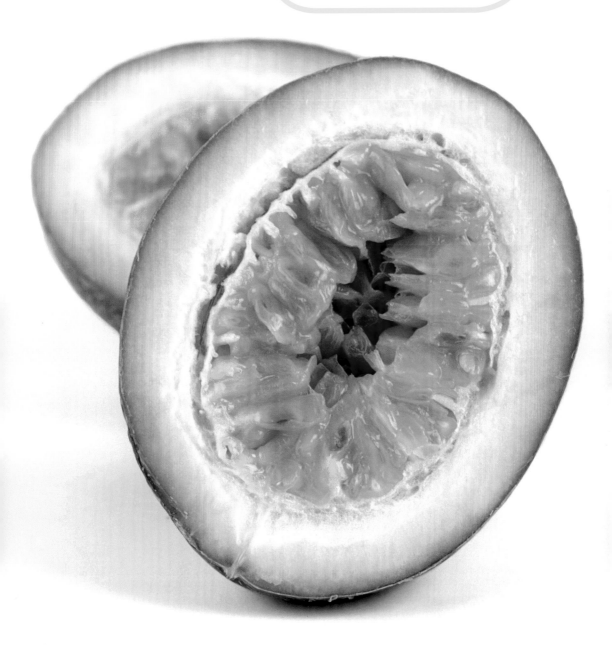

The maracuyá, or passion fruit, is a tart fruit that grows in Peru.

familiar. This incredibly fragrant fruit was a favorite of the Inca, and is still a national favorite. Lúcumas have a thick green skin and sweet orange flesh that tastes like maple syrup.

Camu camus (CAH-moo CAH-moos) are also popular. These little fruits look a lot like purple grapes, and are loaded with vitamin C. They have a tangy flavor and a sweet aroma. Maracuyás (mah-rah-coo-YAHS), or passion fruits, are other favorites. Their jelly-like yellow pulp has a slightly tart flavor and an exotic aroma. Granadas (grah-NAH-dahs) are another local treat. They have a beautiful deep-pink color and a sweet acidic taste.

Peruvians use these and other fruits in puddings, jellies, cakes, and pies. They flock to jugerias (hoo-gay-REE-ahs), or juice stands, where vendors turn fruit into delicious juices, batidos (bah-TEE-dohs), or smoothies, and sweetened juice drinks known as refrescos (ray-FRAYS-cohs). To make juices, vendors mix fresh fruit with ice in a blender. Sugar is added to make a refresco. Either milk or yogurt is added for a batido. Juices, refrescos, and batidos can feature one fruit or a combination. Some Peruvian jugerias serve up more than 90 different combinations. And, because fruit contains lots of vital nutrients, these drinks are both delicious and healthy.

Television host and chef David Jesson explains: "I will never forget the first time I tasted a refresco made from maracuyá. Its taste rivaled that of any other fruit-flavored juice I had tasted. I thought anything that tastes this good has to be bad for you, and although it has to

Pineapple-Strawberry Batido

Batidos and refrescos are favorite Peruvian thirst quenchers. Batidos contain milk. Refrescos do not. Any type of fruit or combination of fruits can be used to make a batido or a refresco. This batido recipe uses pineapple and strawberries. For a sweeter drink, add more sugar.

Ingredients
½ cup diced pineapple
½ cup diced strawberries
1 cup cold water
1 cup milk
1 tablespoon sugar
ice to fill blender

Directions
Put all the ingredients in a blender. Mix until the drink is smooth.
Serves 2.

Any fruit can be used to make a delicious batido or refresco.

Peruvian Crafts

Throughout its long history, Peru has been the home of fine craftspeople. Ancient Peruvians, like the Moche people, created detailed ceremonial cups and woven cloths with pictures that told stories about their daily life and festive events. The Inca had specially chosen women who spent their lives weaving intricate capes made from feathers.

Works of art made out of gold and silver were also an Incan specialty. The first Spaniards to see the Incan Temple of the Sun in Cusco described the courtyard as being filled with life-size llamas, birds, and flowers made of gold. The Inca also made murals of gold, as well as gold eating utensils and jewelry.

Modern Peruvian artists continue the fine work of their ancestors. Peru is known for its fine cloths and intricate textiles, knitted items, baskets, ceramics, leather goods, and beautiful jewelry.

be sweetened with sugar, … maracuyá … is loaded with vitamins and minerals."[9]

Exotic Ice Cream

Peruvian ice cream, too, takes advantage of these delicious fruits. Besides offering traditional flavors like vanilla and chocolate, Peruvian ice cream parlors offer dozens of exotic fruit-flavored ice cream, such as pineapple, banana, lúcuma, tuna, which is the fruit of the prickly pear cactus, mango and its cousin taperiba (tah-pay-REE-bah), and custard-like chirimoya (chee-ree-

MOH-yah), to name just a few. One shop in Lima sells 80 different flavors on a rotating basis.

Peruvian ice cream parlors are usually crowded. They are a favorite meeting place for Peruvians, who sit at little tables eating their ice cream while visiting with friends.

According to writer Marie-Louise Saina, "On any given day, you will find that the popular ice cream parlors are brimming with people who enjoy a long chat while savoring a frozen dessert. … You will find an abundance of unique flavors from the jungle. … Lúcuma is one of the country's top exotic ice cream flavors, and it happens to be my number one choice."[10]

Turning Fog into Drinking Water

More than 1 million people living in Lima, Peru, do not have running water. They can have water delivered by trucks, but the cost is high and many poor Peruvians cannot afford it.

Scientists have found a way to help these people. They erected five specially constructed large nets on a mountaintop in Lima near one neighborhood that lacks running water. The nets catch fog, which is an everyday occurrence in Lima during the winter. As fog passes through the nets, water droplets are deposited on the nets. The water drips down the nets into pits below them. Each net collects about 16 gallons (60.57 liters) of water each night. The water is treated with water-purification tablets. Local people use it for drinking, cooking, and gardening.

Picarónes

Tropical fruits like lúcuma are not the only natural ingredients in Peruvian treats. Pumpkin, squash, and/or sweet potatoes are the main ingredient in picarónes, doughnut-like pastries that are sold all over Peru. Similar fritters are popular in Spain. Spanish settlers brought the recipe to Peru, where pumpkin, squash, or sweet potatoes were added to sweeten the dough.

To make picarónes, bakers make dough from eggs, flour, yeast, spices like cinnamon and nutmeg, and mashed pumpkin, squash, or sweet potatoes, which they shape into thin rings. The rings are dropped into hot oil and are fried until they are crisp and golden on the outside, and soft and flaky inside. Peruvians eat them straight out of the frying pan drenched in sweet, sticky syrup made from **chancaca** (chahn-CAH-cah), a kind of hard brown sugar.

Picarónes taste sweet and spicy and are both crispy and moist at the same time. They smell similar to pumpkin pie.

"Though not the healthiest snack in the world, they are delicious," explains Jason, an American who once lived in Peru. "One of our family's Cusco traditions is to go out for picarones."[11]

Sweet Milk Caramel

Other Peruvian treats depend on **manjar blanco** (mahn-HAR BLAHN-coh), or sweetened caramelized milk, for their sugary taste. Also known as dulce de

Desserts made with manjar blanco, such as this liquid fudge dessert, are the favorites among Peruvians.

Instant Alfajores

Here is a very easy way to make alfajores using ready-made cookies and canned dulce de leche, which is sold in most supermarkets. This recipe uses 2-inch (5cm) cookies. Larger cookies will need more dulce de leche and coconut flakes.

Ingredients
24 butter cookies
¼ to ⅓ cup dulce de leche
4 teaspoons unsweetened coconut flakes

Directions
1. Put the dulce de leche in a bowl. Put the coconut flakes in another bowl.
2. Cover a cookie sheet with nonstick foil.
3. Put a cookie face down on the cookie sheet.
4. Spread a thick layer (about 1 teaspoon) of dulce de leche on the cookie. Press another cookie face up on top of the cookie. Spread a little dulce de leche on the sides of the cookie. Roll the sides in coconut. Repeat with each cookie.

Makes 24 cookies.

Alfajores are a traditional sweet treat in Peru.

leche (DOOL-say day LAY-chay) or natillas (nah-TEE-yas), manjar blanco is a thick creamy caramel sauce made by slowly heating milk and chancaca. Making it requires time and patience. Cooks must constantly stir the mixture until the milk caramelizes. This usually takes about an hour. Ready-made canned versions of manjar blanco make it easy for busy Peruvians to enjoy this traditional treat.

Peruvians love manjar blanco. They use it to fill cakes, pies, crepes, and pastries. They turn it into custards and white fudge. And, spreading it on a hot roll or a slice of toast is a favorite after-school snack. Author Maria Baez Kijac calls it "the most popular and beloved sweet in Latin America."[12]

One of the most popular ways Peruvians use manjar blanco is as a filling for alfajores, a favorite sandwich cookie. The word "alfajor" means delicacy or fancy sweet in Arabic. The Moors, North African people who settled in Spain in the 8th century, brought the recipe to Spain. Spanish nuns took it, along with many other pastry recipes, to Peru.

The cookie consists of two round flaky butter cookies dusted with powdered sugar and filled with creamy sweet manjar blanco. Some cooks also spread manjar blanco along the sides of the cookie and then roll it in grated coconut and/or melted chocolate. With or without coconut and chocolate, the cookies taste crisp when they are first baked, but soften as they age. Some people like to eat them right out of the oven, but many others prefer to wait a few days so that the texture of the filling and the pastry match. Such cookies, according to writer Kathleen Brennan, are "tender, crumbly, perfectly sweet gems."[13]

And, for those people who cannot get enough of alfajores, there are "King Kongs," giant alfajores filled with both manjar blanco and either fruit paste or nut butter. King Kongs are a handful. They are about as big and thick as a quarter-pound hamburger loaded with toppings.

"King Kong," explains authors Joan Peterson and Brook Soltvedt, "may be thought of as alfajores on steroids. This gargantuan treat lives up to its name. It has enormous cookies layered with fillings of manjar blanco, sweet peanut cream or a variety of fruit pastes (… fig or pineapple). It may be round or square with soft or crunchy cookies, a single filling or multiple fillings."[14]

Clearly, when Peruvians want something sweet to eat, they have lots of choices—big or little pastries, liquid or solid treats, frosty cold, or piping hot sweets. Bakeries, ice cream parlors, juice stands, street vendors, cafés, and restaurants tempt Peruvians with delicious treats. Whether for a snack or dessert, fresh fruit juices, batidos, and refrescos, rich ice cream in exotic flavors, spicy picarónes, and giant cookies filled with manjar blanco can satisfy any sweet tooth.

chapter 4

Food for Celebrations

Celebrating is a way of life in Peru. Peruvians hold 3,000 festivals each year. Added to these are holidays, special occasions, and family get-togethers. Food plays a key role in each and every event.

Peruvian chef Flavio Solorzano puts it this way: "When you are born, Peruvians eat. When you die, we stand on your grave and eat. In Peru, everything is about food."[15]

Celebrating Christmas

Christmas is one of the most important of all festivities in Peru. The celebration begins on Christmas Eve or Noche Buena (NO-chay BWAY-nah). That is when families gather for Christmas dinner, which tradition-

Humitas are a traditional part of Christmas dinner in Peru. Preparing humitas takes time; many families prepare them together as a part of the tradition.

ally begins with tamales (tah-MAH-lays) or humitas (oo-ME-tahs), as they are also known in Peru. Humitas are steamy corn pockets filled with meat and spices, and wrapped in fresh cornhusks or banana leaves.

Making humitas takes time and energy. The husks, or leaves, must be soaked and cleaned. The corn must be turned into dough. The dough must be kneaded, and the filling must be prepared. Finally, the humitas must be assembled and steamed.

Many Peruvian families get together to prepare humitas early in the day. Young and old pitch in and have fun working together.

Maria Baez Kijac, who grew up in Ecuador where the same tradition is followed, explains: "Whenever I have

Pachamanca

Pachamanca (pah-cha-MAHN-cah) is a Peruvian dish originally created by the Inca to honor the Earth. It is often eaten on special occasions.

To make pachamanca, cooks dig a hole and fill it with wood and volcanic stones instead of regular stones, which can explode at high heat. A fire is lit. It is used to heat the stones. When the stones are very hot, different foods are placed in the hole in layers. First come potatoes. Next come different meats, followed by a layer of chili peppers. Corn, beans, and cheese make up the top layer. The whole thing is topped with more hot stones, and the pit is covered with soil, which prevents heat, smoke, and steam from escaping. The food is left to cook for about two hours. It is served in large bowls, and eaten outside, usually accompanied by music and celebration.

a longing for the foods of my childhood, visions of tamales fill my mind. Maybe it is the memories tamales bring back of holidays and family celebrations and the excitement found in the kitchen, where many loving hands labored together in the preparation of this beloved specialty."[16]

Colorful and Spicy

Peruvian tamales or humitas come in a variety of colors depending on the type of corn used. Traditionally, Peruvians make the dough by freshly grinding corn and mixing it with lots of chili paste. The abundant use

Cheese Zarza

A zarza (ZAR-zah) is a Peruvian chopped salad. It is a popular side dish. Some type of zarza is likely to be served with Christmas dinner. This one features mozzarella cheese.

Ingredients
¼ pound mozzarella cheese, cut into chunks
2 hard-boiled egg, cut into chunks
½ small red onion, diced
1 large ripe tomato, cut into chunks
1 tablespoon sliced black olives
½ teaspoon chopped cilantro
½ teaspoon chopped fresh mint
1 teaspoon lime juice
1 teaspoon olive oil
salt and pepper to taste

Directions
1. Soak the onion pieces in cold water for 20 minutes.
2. Drain the onions. Combine all the ingredients. Mix well.
Serves 2–4

of chili makes Peruvian humitas spicier than those of other Latin American nations. They are also larger and fatter.

Once the dough is ready, cooks place the dough on a banana leaf or cornhusk and spread a filling made of chicken or pork mixed with roasted peanuts, black olives, bits of chili, and hard-boiled eggs down the middle. They fold the dough over the filling and the husk or leaf over the dough to form a plump rectangle, which they tie shut with a bit of twine. Finally, they drop the humitas into a pot of hot water and steam them until they are hot and delicious. They are served wrapped in the leaves, like little holiday packages.

When Peruvians open the little packages, a fragrant cloud of steam greets them. To Peruvians, humitas are the scent and taste of Christmas—moist, fresh, and zesty.

Stuffed Turkey

Most families follow the humitas with a plump, juicy, stuffed turkey. Turkeys are native to the Americas, and Peruvians have been eating them for centuries. However, because many Peruvians do not own an oven and must take the turkey to a local bakery for roasting, Peruvians have come to associate turkeys with special occasions and especially with Christmas. In fact, 50 percent of the turkeys eaten in Peru are consumed at Christmas.

Whether cooks roast the turkey in their own kitchen or take it to the local bakery, they have to prepare the turkey before it goes into the oven. Some cooks marinate the bird in fruit juice seasoned with chili powder before roasting it. Others rub the turkey with butter, chili powder, and salt. Stuffing, too, varies. Different combinations of ground meat, ham, onions, carrots, whole apples, dried fruit, hard-boiled eggs, nuts, and olives spiced with chili, cinnamon, and nutmeg are most popular. To crown the turkey, some cooks decorate it with pineapple slices. The juice from the pineapple moistens the turkey, while the acid tenderizes it. The end result is a luscious moist bird with a unique sweet, salty, spicy flavor and an exotic fruity aroma. It is, according to author Marks, "the star of the Christmas cena [SAY-na, meaning dinner]."[17]

The turkey is usually accompanied by different salads, applesauce, hot chocolate, and **panettóne** (pahnay-TONE), a tall, soft, airy, sweet bread filled with dried fruit that Italian immigrants brought to Peru.

During the holiday season, brightly colored boxes of the bread line supermarket and bakery shelves. Peruvians eat over 2 tons (1.8 metric tons) of panettóne during the Christmas season. The sweet bread is so much a part of Peruvian Christmas celebrations that holiday guests rarely arrive for Christmas dinner without a gift-wrapped loaf.

Panettóne is a sweet bread that can be found at Christmas celebrations throughout Peru.

Chocolate and Charity

Drinking hot chocolate during the Christmas season is a tradition in Peru. At Christmastime, wealthy families, church groups, and businesses throughout Peru spread holiday cheer by sponsoring chocolatadas (cho-coh-lah-TAH-dahs) for poor children. Some groups also hold chocolatadas for elderly people in need.

Chocolatadas are Christmas parties in which needy children are served cups of hot chocolate, panettóne, and candy. There is usually singing, dancing, games, little skits, a Christmas tree, and decorations. The children are given a toy, and sometimes a new piece of clothing. Often, a community member dresses as Papa Noel, the Peruvian version of Santa Claus, and delivers the gifts. Many poor families come from rural areas to towns and cities just so they can attend a chocolatada.

Carnival Meats

Carnival (car-nee-VAHL) is another festive Peruvian event. It is a street party that lasts from three days to one week. It occurs right before Lent, the 40-day period before Easter. For religious reasons, many Peruvians give up meat during Lent, so as one last time to indulge before fasting, Peruvians hold Carnival, with parades, bands, floats, dances, and lots of special foods, especially meat. In fact the root of the Spanish word "Carnival" is carne (CAR-nay), meaning meat.

Puchero (poo-CHAY-roh), a rich and filling stew loaded with meat, is a Carnival favorite. Carnival partic-

Puchero is a rich, meaty stew that is traditionally served during Carnival, a festival that occurs right before Lent, the 40-day period before Easter.

ipants look forward to the last day of Carnival, known as Fat Tuesday, because that is the day street vendors prepare this popular dish. Puchero contains many meats including pork, chicken, beef heart, lamb's head, and sausage.

The meat is slowly cooked in water and spices. When it is tender, it is removed from the pot, and potatoes, yuca, and corn are added. Whole peaches, rice, chickpeas, and cabbage are cooked in separate pots.

Puchero is served on a platter with each ingredient in a traditional spot. The meat is in the middle. The rice mixed with the chickpeas top the meat. The corn, the yuca and potatoes, and the peaches surround it. The whole thing is topped with cabbage leaves and served

Arroz con Leche

Arroz con leche (ah-ROHS cohn LAY-chay), or rice pudding, is a favorite Peruvian dessert. It is often served at family gatherings and special events. It is not difficult to make.

Ingredients
½ cup short grain rice
4 cups condensed or whole milk
½ cup sugar
pinch of salt
2 cinnamon sticks
1 teaspoon vanilla
⅓ cup raisins
ground cinnamon to taste

Directions
1. Put milk, rice, salt, and cinnamon sticks in a large pot. Bring the mixture to a boil over medium heat.
2. Reduce the heat and cook on low uncovered until most of the liquid is absorbed and the pudding is thick and creamy, about 45 minutes. Stir often.
3. Add the sugar, vanilla, and raisins. Cook on low for 10 minutes. Stir often.
4. Remove the pot from the heat. Remove the cinnamon sticks. Put the pudding in a bowl, sprinkle the top with ground cinnamon and refrigerate. Serve chilled.

Serves 4.

Arroz con leche is best served chilled.

with salsa and a bowl of the stewing liquid. The meat and vegetables taste buttery soft, but not mushy. And, the different flavors—sweet, earthy, meaty, and starchy—blend together so that no one flavor overwhelms the others. The taste, says Peruvian food writer Rosario Olivas Weston, is "delicious and comforting."[18]

Purple Month

October brings more delicious festive foods. It is known as mes morado (mace moh-RAH-doh), or purple month. During October, Peruvians honor the Lord of Miracles, a 350-year-old image of Jesus Christ that miraculously survived a devastating 17th century earthquake when everything around it was destroyed. Huge processions are held during the month in which devoted followers wearing purple robes carry replicas of the image. A special pastry known as turrón de Doña Pepa (toor-ROHN de DOHN-ya PAY-pah) is sold everywhere.

According to legend, Doña Pepa was a 17th century black slave whose arm was paralyzed. She prayed to the Lord of Miracles to heal her. Amazingly, she regained use of her arm. As an act of thanks, she made a pastry, which she took to the procession. It consisted of layers of **nougat**, a paste made of sesame seeds, flour, butter, egg yolks, and anise, a black licorice–like spice, held together with sticky syrup and topped with brightly colored bits of candy.

The main ingredient in the syrup was chancaca (chahn-CAH-cah), which was combined with water, cinnamon, and tiny pieces of pineapple, peaches, or-

Turrón de Doña Pepa is a special pastry that is prepared in October to honor the Lord of Miracles.

anges, and lime. The sweet fruity confection became known as turrón de Doña Pepa. Peruvians have associated it with purple month ever since.

Pico, who lived in Peru, explains: "What I miss the most of the October festivities is the Turrón de Doña Pepa. ... The memories have me salivating."[19]

There is no doubt that celebratory foods bring to mind many happy memories for Peruvians. They make festivals and holidays more special and more fun.

Metric conversions

Mass (weight)

1 ounce (oz.)	= 28.0 grams (g)
8 ounces	= 227.0 grams
1 pound (lb.) or 16 ounces	= 0.45 kilograms (kg)
2.2 pounds	= 1.0 kilogram

Liquid Volume

1 teaspoon (tsp.)	= 5.0 milliliters (ml)
1 tablespoon (tbsp.)	= 15.0 milliliters
1 fluid ounce (oz.)	= 30.0 milliliters
1 cup (c.)	= 240 milliliters
1 pint (pt.)	= 480 milliliters
1 quart (qt.)	= 0.96 liters (l)
1 gallon (gal.)	= 3.84 liters

Pan Sizes

8- inch cake pan	= 20 x 4-centimeter cake pan
9-inch cake pan	= 23 x 3.5-centimeter cake pan
11 x 7-inch baking pan	= 28 x 18-centimeter baking pan
13 x 9-inch baking pan	= 32.5 x 23-centimeter baking pan
9 x 5-inch loaf pan	= 23 x 13-centimeter loaf pan
2-quart casserole	= 2-liter casserole

Temperature

212° F	= 100° C (boiling point of water)
225° F	= 110° C
250° F	= 120° C
275° F	= 135° C
300° F	= 150° C
325° F	= 160° C
350° F	= 180° C
375° F	= 190° C
400° F	= 200° C

Length

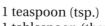

1/4 inch (in.)	= 0.6 centimeters (cm)
1/2 inch	= 1.25 centimeters
1 inch	= 2.5 centimeters

Notes

Chapter 1: A Diverse Land

1. Quoted in Laura Fraser, "Next Stop Lima," *Gourmet Magazine*, August 2006, p.106.

2. Alvaro Ruiz de Somocurcio, "Cuzco: The Sacred Valley, Blessed Land," Living in Peru. www.livinginperu.com/gastronomy/features-538.

3. Maria Baez Kijac, *The South American Table.* Boston: Harvard Common Press, 2003, p. 332.

4. Copeland Marks, *The Exotic Kitchens of Peru.* Lanham, MD: M. Evans, 1999, p. 63.

5. Marks, *The Exotic Kitchens of Peru*, p. 59.

Chapter 2: A Cultural Blend

6. Quoted in Rachel Brooks-Ames, "Ceviche—South America Offers the Next Big Thing in Raw Food," January 21, 2010, Latin America News Dispatch. http://latindispatch.com/2010/01/21/feature-ceviche-south-america-offers-the-next-big-thing-in-raw-food/.

7. Mariella Mazzei, "Chifa, Magical Food Result of Chinese Immigration in Peru," Living in Peru. www.livinginperu.com/gastronomy/features-1093.

8. Matt Villano, "The Delicacy of the Andes," July 23, 2007, World Hum. www.worldhum.com/features/travel-stories/the_delicacy_of_the_andes_20070723/.

Chapter 3: A Sweet Tooth

9. David Jesson, "Peru Alive with Fresh Juices and Creative Refreshments," Living in Peru. http://livinginperu.com/gastronomy/features-181.

10. Marie-Louise Saina, "I Scream … for Ice Cream!" November 17, 2009, Living in Peru. www.livinginperu.com/features-996-cuisine-i-screama-for-icd-cream.

11. Jason, "Delicious Picarónes," October 22, 2009, Alpaca Suitcase. http://alpaca-suitcase.blogspot.com/2009/10/picarones.html.

12. Kijac, *The South American Table*, p. 390.

13. Kathleen Brennan, "A Sweet to Smile For," Saveur.com. www.saveur.com/article/kitche/A-sweet-to-Smile-For.

14. Joan Peterson and Brook Soltvedt, *Eat Smart in Peru*. Madison, WI: Gingko, 2006, p. 33.

Chapter 4: Food for Celebrations

15. Quoted in Chris Martell, "Diverse Crops, Cooking Methods and Cultures Make Peru's Menu a Melting Pot," March 5, 2010, 77 Square. http://host.madison.com/entertainment/dining/article_e4b53945-1601-5a6a-9aaa-03e39bbd8ef0.html.

16. Kijac, *The South American Table*, p. 81.

17. Marks, *The Exotic Kitchens of Peru*, p.198.

18. Rosario Olivas Weston, "The Culinary Empire," *Chasqui*, (Cultural Bulletin of the Ministry of Foreign Affairs), December 2009, p. 8.

19. Quoted in Barbara Drake, "Purple Month Strikes Again," October 7, 2009, An American in Lima. http://americaninlima.com/2009/10/07/purple-month-strikes-again/.

Glossary

ají: Peruvian word for chili peppers.

ceviche: A fish dish made by marinating fish in lime juice. (Also spelled cebiche or seviche.)

chancaca: A type of brown sugar.

chifa: Peruvian-Chinese style of cooking.

choclo: Peruvian word for corn.

chuño: Freeze-dried potatoes.

conquistador: A Spanish explorer who came to the Americas seeking gold and riches.

cuy: Peruvian word for guinea pig.

Inca: A group of native South American people who ruled a large empire from the 12th to the mid-16th centuries, whose capital was in Cusco, Peru.

llama: A domesticated South American animal related to camels with a wooly coat.

lúcumas: Tropical fruit native to Peru.

manjar blanco: Caramel cream popular in Peru.

nougat: A chewy sweet made with sugar or honey, nuts or seeds, and/or dried fruit.

panettóne: A tall sweet bread similar to fruitcake.

pre-Columbian: Time before the arrival of Christopher Columbus to the Americas.

puree: To turn solid food into a soft moist paste.

salsa: Spicy sauce usually made of peppers, onions, and spices.

For Further Exploration

Books

Sandy Donovan, *Teens in Peru*. Mankato: MN: Compass Point, 2008. Examines the daily life of Peruvian teens.

Kieran Falconer, Lynette Quek, *Peru*. New York: Benchmark, 2006. Looks at Peruvian religion, art, food, leisure activities, and culture.

Jane Shuter, *The Incas*. Chicago: Heinemann, 2008. Explores Incan civilization and daily life.

Web Sites

Food in Every Country, "Peru," (www.foodbycountry .com/Kazakhstan-to-South-Africa/Peru.html). This site provides information about Peru's geography, environment, history, food, special events, and mealtime customs, with pictures and recipes.

National Geographic Kids, "Peru," (http://kids .nationalgeographic.com/kids/places/find/peru/). Readers will find facts about Peru's geography, history, culture, and wildlife with colored photos, a video, maps, and an e-postcard.

Time for Kids, "Around the World, Peru,"

(www.timeforkids.com/TFK/kids/hh/goplaces/main/0,28375,602932,00.html). Take a virtual trip to Peru with information, photos, a history time line and postcards.

Yahoo Kids! "World Factbook," (http://kids.yahoo.com/reference/world-factbook/country/pe—Peru#main). Lots of information about Peru's geography, government, people, economy, and challenges the nation faces, with a flag and map.

Index

Picture credits

About the Author

Barbara Sheen is the author of more than 50 books for young people. She lives in New Mexico with her family. In her spare time, she likes to swim, walk, garden, and read. Of course, she loves to cook!